THE *Missing* SHOP MANUAL

SHAPER

D1608034

THE *Missing* **SHOP MANUAL**

SHAPER

{ the tool information you need at your fingertips }

Distributed By
Fox Chapel Publishing

FOX CHAPEL
PUBLISHING

© 2011 by Skills Institute Press LLC
"Missing Shop Manual" series trademark of Skills Institute Press
Published and distributed in North America by Fox Chapel Publishing Company, Inc.

Shaper is an original work, first published in 2011.

Portions of text and art previously published by and reproduced under license with Direct Holdings Americas Inc.

ISBN 978-1-56523-494-9

Library of Congress Cataloging-in-Publication Data

Shaper.
    p. cm. -- (The missing shop manual)
Includes index.
ISBN 978-1-56523-494-9
1. Woodworking tools. I. Fox Chapel Publishing.

TT186.S448 2011
684'.082--dc22

2010017536

To learn more about the other great books from Fox Chapel Publishing, or to find a retailer near you, call toll-free 800-457-9112 or visit us at **www.FoxChapelPublishing.com**.

Note to Authors: We are always looking for talented authors to write new books in our area of woodworking, design, and related crafts. Please send a brief letter describing your idea to Acquisition Editor, 1970 Broad Street, East Petersburg, PA 17520.

Printed in China
First printing: February 2011

Contents

WHAT YOU WILL LEARN

Chapter 1
The Shaper 8

Chapter 2
Cutters and Accessories 14

Chapter 3
Setup and Safety 20

Chapter 4
Basic Cuts 30

Chapter 5
Vacuum Jigs 44

Chapter 6
Frame-and-Panel Doors 48

CHAPTER 1:

The Shaper

The shaper and the router share a common heritage. In the mid-19th century an inventor in Ohio produced a prototype for a machine with a vertical spindle projecting out of a horizontal table. This machine, known as a spindle router, was virtually identical to the present-day shaper. Another model from the same era, employing an overhead spindle to raise panels and cut grooves and recesses, evolved into today's router.

Similar origins notwithstanding, the router and shaper have since followed different paths. The router is often considered the most useful and versatile woodworking power tool; the shaper, on the other hand, is frequently the last machine added to the woodworking shop, a fact that belies its usefulness to the craftsman.

If you frequently cut decorative moldings in the edges of curved workpieces, or if you build many

The shaper is a common sight in production shops, where it is unequaled for constructing cabinet doors. The panel-raising jig shown above allows arched top rails and arched raised panels to be shaped quickly, safely, and accurately.

doors and drawers, the shaper is an ideal tool for your shop. Basically, the machine is a bigger, stronger, and more stable version of a table-mounted router, with a much wider range of available cutters. Shaper cutters *(page 14)* vary from simple, single profile cutters to complex combination systems that produce the contours of a host of individual blades. Relatively safe and easy to work with, solid cutters with carbide teeth are the preferred choice, though many woodworkers still opt for the versatility of grinding their own knives to whatever profile they desire.

With its large cutter exposed above the table, the shaper requires special attention to safety; the tool is often considered to be the most dangerous machine in the shop. Key concerns are the rotation of the spindle, the direction of feed, and the location of the cutter with regard to the workpiece. Most shaper spindles and cutters are designed to rotate either clockwise or counterclockwise; each direction offers its own advantages and disadvantages. Most cutters are designed to cut from above a workpiece while spinning counterclockwise (as seen from above). This offers a better view of the cut and, because of the direction of the threads on the spindle, ensures that the nut securing the cutter in place remains tight throughout the operation. By reversing spindle rotation and inverting the cutter so that it lies mostly below table level, you can shape the underside of the workpiece. This is often a safer setup for freehand shaping or for working with extra-wide or very long stock. If the workpiece lifts up, the cutter will not gouge it and kick the board back.

Read your owner's manual carefully and follow the setup and cutting guidelines discussed here, starting on page 20. Take the time to build the guards and fence shown on pages 24 and 26; they will make your machine much safer to use.

ANATOMY OF A SHAPER

The shaper works very much like a table-mounted router, but it is larger, heavier, and generally more powerful. The heart of the machine is its spindle, a threaded ½- to 1¼-inch-diameter assembly that typically turns a cutter from 7,000 to 10,000 rpm. The spindle, in turn, is driven by a belt- or direct-drive mechanism connected to a ½- to 5-horsepower motor. Some models offer variable speeds.

Shapers are sized by spindle diameter. Machines with larger-diameter spindles require more powerful motors, but these tools vibrate less, produce cleaner cuts, and can be used with a wider assortment of cutters. Many shapers feature interchangeable spindles.

Shaper cutters and accessories are secured to the spindle with a nut and lock washer. The spindle normally turns counterclockwise. On many machines, spindle rotation can be reversed by flicking a switch located on the motor junction box. This is a valuable feature, allowing stock to be fed from either side of the table.

ANATOMY OF A SHAPER *(continued)*

Fence assembly
Guides work across table for straight cuts; split into two halves that can be individually adjusted and locked in position.

Table insert ring
One of a set of concentric rings set in table to accept different diameter cutters, maximizing table bearing surface.

Spindle height adjustment handwheel
Raises and lowers spindle assembly to set cutter height.

Height adjustment lock knob
Fixes height of spindle assembly; must be tightened before shaper is operated.

Ring guard
Mounted on spindle to protect operator's fingers from cutter; remains stationary as cutter spins. Made of clear plastic to keep cutting operations visible.

Spindle assembly
Reversible, with a ¾-inch spindle at one end and a ½-inch spindle at the other; mounted to a bracket under the table.

Switch arm
Can be swung out of the way to accommodate large workpieces.

On/off switch
Toggle bracket accepts padlock to prevent accidental start-up.

Starting pin
A steel rod that supports work until it contacts rub bearing for freehand cuts; fits into hole in table on infeed side of cutter.

Front access panel
Covers motor and drive mechanism; removed to access spindle speed adjustment.

ANATOMY OF A SHAPER *(continued)*

Depending on the model, the height of the spindle can be adjusted from 2 to 6 inches.

Few cuts on the shaper are made without an accessory or a jig. Most shaper tables feature a miter gauge slot. Straight cuts should be guided by the fence or a miter gauge. While some fences are comprised of two solid arms that can be moved close to the cutters, the

This portable ⅞-horsepower bench top shaper can perform most of the functions of a larger tool. It is equipped with a ½-inch spindle and an accessory router chuck, and can turn cutters and router bits at 9,000 rpm.

type of fence shown at right has segments that slide laterally to conform more closely to the cutter shape, providing an extra measure of safety. Curved work can be shaped with a jig, or a template or starting pin used in conjunction with a rub bearing, which must be mounted on the spindle.

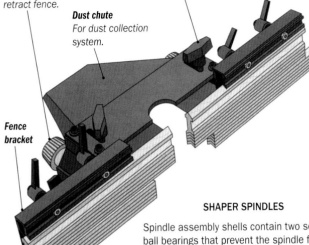

Fence locking handle
Attached to fence locking rod; tightened to secure fence in position on table to width of cut.

Fence segment locking handle
Locks fence segments at desired setting.

Fence adjustment knob
Turned to advance or retract fence.

Dust chute
For dust collection system.

Fence bracket

Fence segments
Individual wooden fingers adjust to frame cutter and ring guard, increasing fence bearing surface and protecting operator's fingers.

SHAPER SPINDLES

Spindle assembly shells contain two sets of ball bearings that prevent the spindle from deflecting during a cut. Both assemblies shown below are double-ended. The standard assembly *(below, top)* can accommodate different-sized shaper cutters, depending on which end is used; the router/stub adapter assembly *(below, bottom)* accepts router bits at one end and ½-inch-bore cutters at the

Spindle assembly

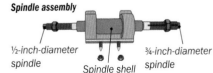

½-inch-diameter spindle

Spindle shell

¾-inch-diameter spindle

Router/stub adapter spindle assembly

Router collet

Stub spindle

CHAPTER 2

Cutters and Accessories

Carving decorative molding with a shaper used to involve grinding steel knives to the desired profile in the shop.

The knives were inserted into slotted cutterheads and held in place by friction—an arrangement notorious for releasing the cutters with disastrous results.

Today, the knives are ground commercially and normally secured to the cutterhead with hex bolts. (In fact, you should avoid using an assembled cutterhead on a shaper unless it features a method of fixing the knives in place.) Most knives are made from high-speed steel (HSS) and are available in a variety of profiles. If you have a profile in mind that you cannot find in a catalog and are unable to grind in your own shop, check with a manufacturer of cutters. Some companies will grind knives to your specifications.

More often, two-and three-wing solid shaper

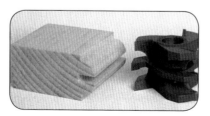

Cutter sets provide a precise method of making snug-fitting joints for frame-and-panel construction. The cut produced by this sticking cutter will mate with the profile carved by its coping counterpart.

cutters are used by woodworkers. These are usually HSS cutters, tipped with tungsten carbide to provide a more durable cutting edge. Most solid cutters are sold in standard bore sizes from $\frac{1}{2}$ to $\frac{1}{4}$ inches. As shown below, they come in a variety of profiles, from standard detail cutters used for molding to cutter sets like cope-and-stick assemblies.

SHAPER CUTTER PROFILES

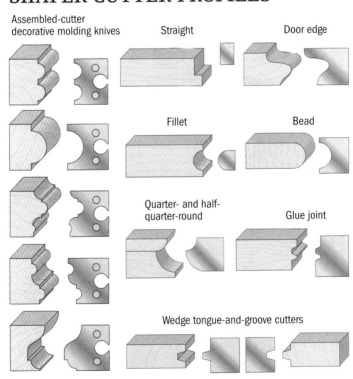

Assembled-cutter decorative molding knives

Straight

Door edge

Fillet

Bead

Quarter- and half-quarter-round

Glue joint

Wedge tongue-and-groove cutters

SHAPER CUTTERS

Four types of shaper cutters: (clockwise from top right) an assembled cutter, a three-knife safety cutter, a detail cutter, and a cutter set.

Any shaper cutter will create a different profile according to the thickness of the workpiece and the height of the cutter on the spindle. Make several test cuts before shaping a workpiece. For combination systems and cutter sets, follow the manufacturer's instructions.

You should also refer to the manufacturer's specifications for the required spindle size and maximum rpm rating for a cutter. And although you can use bushings to fit large-bore cutters on small-diameter spindles, the added stress may cause the spindle to deflect.

The quality of your shaper work depends to a great extent on the cutters. Never use a damaged or rusted cutter. Keep cutting edges sharp and wipe them clean after each use. Carbide cutters can be chipped easily, so take care when storing them.

SHAPER CUTTERS *(continued)*

Door lip

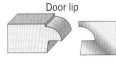

Cope-and-stick

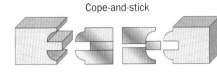

Horizontal panel-raising

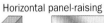
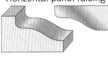

Cope-and-stick (Cove-and-bead style)

Roman ogee

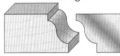

Drawer lock

Lock miter

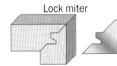

Horizontal panel-raising and back

SHAPER ACCESSORIES

Tenoner
Holds stock on end for shaping; features bar that slides in table miter slot.

Hold-down rods
Mounted to fence on infeed and outfeed sides of cutter to press work firmly against fence and table; adjustable to accommodate various sizes of stock.

Bushings
Inserted in hole of cutter to allow large-bore cutters to fit on small-diameter spindles; used in pairs, with one on each side of cutter.

Rub bearing
Mounted on spindle above or below cutter to provide a bearing surface for edge of workpiece or template; available in different sizes to accommodate various cutter diameters and achieve precise depths of cut.

Push block and push stick
For feeding stock along shaper fence. Push block (top) has rubber base to grip workpiece; push stick (bottom) guides narrow stock.

Shim
Installed on spindle to make small height adjustments to cutter.

Miter gauge
Guides workpiece across table; used principally for shaping end grain. Features hold downs to clamp stock face down; additional hold-down screws can be installed on jig.

SHAPER ACCESSORIES *(continued)*

Spacers
Mounted on spindle to separate cutters from guard or rub bearing.

Spacer collar
Placed on spindle to set cutter at desired location.

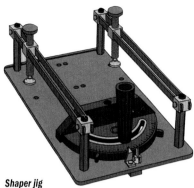
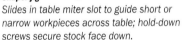

Shaper jig
Slides in table miter slot to guide short or narrow workpieces across table; hold-down screws secure stock face down.

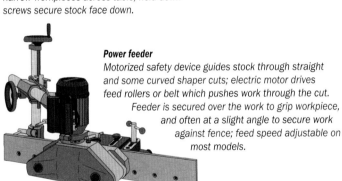

Power feeder
Motorized safety device guides stock through straight and some curved shaper cuts; electric motor drives feed rollers or belt which pushes work through the cut. Feeder is secured over the work to grip workpiece, and often at a slight angle to secure work against fence; feed speed adjustable on most models.

CHAPTER 3

Setup and Safety

Few woodworking machines require as much attention to safety as the shaper.

Its high-speed cutters are difficult to guard fully and they are prone to kickback.

Before beginning any shaping operation, make sure the spindle is fastened securely to the machine and its height is locked. Turn the spindle by hand to make sure the cutter turns with the spindle. Any spindle vibration or vertical or lateral motion during a cut can spell trouble. Replace the spindle bearings or the entire assembly if you notice any problems. Periodically perform the test on the next page to ensure the spindle shaft turns true.

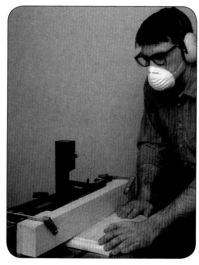

Personal safety gear, such as safety glasses, dust mask, and hearing protection, should be worn for all shaping operations. In addition, the extra-wide featherboard clamped to the fence for this cut helps prevent kickback by keeping the workpiece flat on the table.

CHECKING THE SPINDLE

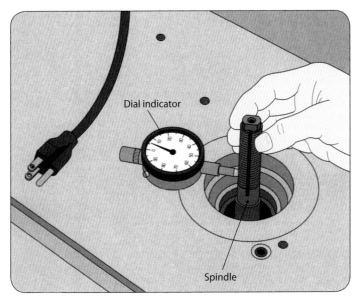

Dial indicator

Spindle

Testing for runout

Set a magnetic-base dial indicator face up on the shaper table so the plunger of the device contacts the spindle. Calibrate the gauge to zero according to the manufacturer's instructions. Then turn the spindle slowly by hand *(above)*. The dial indicator will register spindle runout—the amount of wobble that the spindle would transmit to a cutter. Perform the test at intervals along the length of the spindle, adjusting its height by ½ inch each time. If the runout exceeds 0.005 inch for any of the tests, replace the spindle.

CHANGING A CUTTER

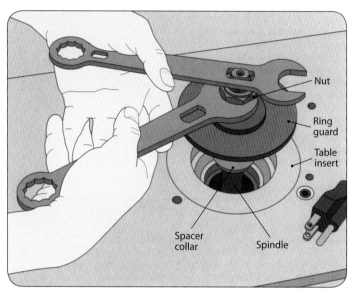

Nut

Ring
guard

Table
insert

Spacer
collar

Spindle

Tightening the cutter on the spindle

Place the appropriate insert ring in the table to support the workpiece.
Slide a spacer collar on the spindle so the cutter assembly will sit near
the bottom of the shaft, while allowing for a sufficient range of height
adjustment. For a freehand cut, mount a rub bearing next. Then slide
on the cutter and ring guard. You may need to place a spacer collar
on both sides of the cutter to ensure the rub bearing and guard spin
freely on the spindle; the cutter should be as close to the bearing as
possible without touching it. Slip on another spacer collar, then add the
lock washer and nut. Tighten the nut using the two wrenches supplied
with the shaper. Hold the spindle steady with one wrench and tighten
with the other. For extra leverage, position the wrenches so that you can
squeeze them together *(above)*.

CHANGING A CUTTER *(continued)*

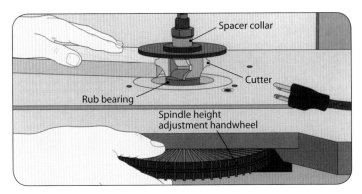

Spacer collar

Cutter

Rub bearing

Spindle height
adjustment handwheel

Setting the cutter height

Once the cutter has been installed, butt the workpiece against the
cutter. Turn the spindle height adjustment hand-wheel to set the cutting
edges to the appropriate height *(above)*. Clockwise raises the spindle;
counterclockwise lowers it. To eliminate any play from the handwheel,
turn it counterclockwise slightly, then clockwise to the correct setting. Fix
the spindle height with the height adjustment lock knob. Make a test cut
in a scrap board and readjust the cutter height, if necessary.

SETTING UP THE FENCE

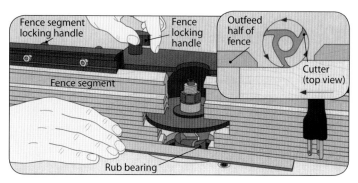

Adjusting the fence

For the model shown, loosen the four fence segment locking handles and move the wooden segments on both halves of the fence as close as possible to the spindle without touching the cutting edges or guard. Lock the handles, then set the width of cut, moving the fence back from the cutter for a wide pass and advancing it for a shallow cut. For a partial cut, where only a portion of the edge of the workpiece will be removed, loosen the fence locking handles. Then hold a straightedge against the fence and move both halves as a unit until the straightedge contacts the rub bearing *(above)*. Tighten the handles. If you are making a full cut, in which the cutter will shape the entire edge of the workpiece, turn off the shaper a few inches into the cut. Holding the board in place against the fence, advance the outfeed half until it butts against the cut part of the stock *(inset)*, then finish the pass.

SETTING UP THE FENCE *(continued)*

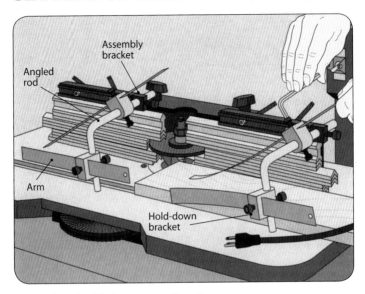

Installing hold downs on the fence

The shaper fence should be used with hold-downs or featherboards whenever possible to keep the workpiece flat against the table and fence. Install a hold-down device on your shaper fence following the manufacturer's instructions. For the spring-type model shown, attach the assembly brackets of the device to the fence brackets, then mount the angled rods on the assembly brackets. Position the metal arms of each rod so that one presses down on the workpiece and the other applies lateral pressure on the stock toward the fence. Lock the arms in place by tightening the hold-down brackets using a hex wrench *(above)*.

TWO SHAPER GUARDS

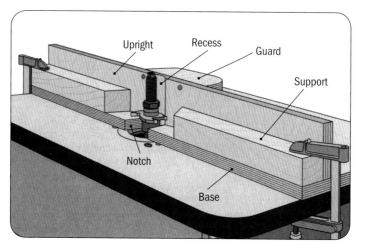

Upright Recess Guard Support Notch Base

The shop-made fence shown above, made from ¾-inch plywood and a few scraps of lumber, is an inexpensive alternative to a commercial fence. It is also very safe, since the cutting edges only project through a narrow slot in the fence and are covered by a guard. Start by cutting the base and upright from plywood. Make both pieces as long as the table; the base should be about 12 inches wide and the upright about 3 inches wide. Before assembling the pieces, cut a notch into the back edge of the base in line with the spindle and carve a recess across the width of the upright's back face; align the recess with the notch. Next, cut the supports from 2-by-2 stock. One end of the supports should be flush with the ends of the base; miter the other end to clear the cutter. Attach the supports to the base, then screw the upright to the supports; countersink your fasteners.

TWO SHAPER GUARDS *(continued)*

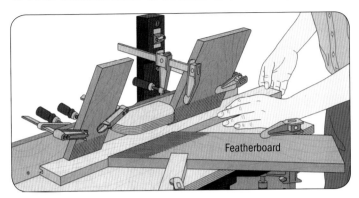

Featherboard

To set up the fence, use a saber saw to cut a precise slot for the cutter. Or, place the fence on the shaper table, clamping only one end in position. With the cutter you plan to use installed on the spindle, turn on the shaper and carefully pivot the free end of the fence into the cutter until the cutting edges rout a slot through the upright and project by the proper amount. Then, turn off the machine and clamp the free end of the fence to the table. Finally, cut a plywood guard large enough to extend over the cutter and screw it to the upright, flush with the top edge.

To make a cut, feed the workpiece into the cutter with both hands, using featherboards to apply pressure against the upright and the base of the fence. Stand toward the front of the machine table, so your body is not in line with the workpiece. This way, if the wood were to be kicked back, it would not hit you.

TWO SHAPER GUARDS *(continued)*

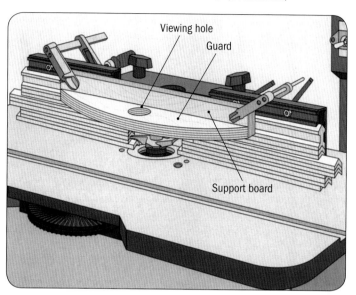

Building a fence-mounted guard

The shaper guard shown above is ideal for fence-guided operations.
Cut the pieces from ¾-inch plywood, making the guard in the shape
of an arc large enough to extend from the fence and shield the cutter
completely. The support board should be wide enough to be clamped
to the fence when the guard is almost touching the spindle. Screw the
guard flush with the bottom edge of the support board; countersink the
fasteners. Next, clamp the jig in position and mark a point on the guard
above the cutter. Remove the jig and bore a 1¼-inch-diameter hole
through the guard at the mark; the hole will allow you to view the cutter
during shaping operations.

TWO SHAPER GUARDS *(continued)*

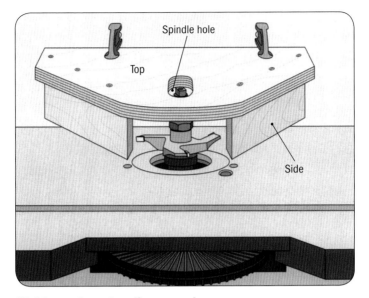

Spindle hole

Top

Side

Making a freestanding guard

For freehand shaping, make a guard like the one shown above. Sawn from
¾-inch plywood, it covers the cutter from the shaper's top, back, and sides.
Cut the top about 16 inches long and wide enough to extend from the back
of the table to about 1½ inches in front of the cutter. Bevel the front ends of
the sides so they can be positioned as close as possible to the cutter. Rip
the sides so the top will sit above the bit with just enough clearance for you
to see the cutter. Hold the top on the table and mark a point on it directly
over the spindle. Cut an oval-shaped hole through the top at the mark, large
enough to clear the spindle and allow you to move the guard across the table
slightly to accommodate different cutters. Fasten the top to the sides with
countersunk screws. To use the guard, position it on the table with the spindle
projecting through the top, and with the sides as close as possible to the
cutting edges. Clamp the guard in place.

CHAPTER 4:
Basic Cuts

Few tools can match the shaper's precision and efficiency for carving decorative contours in wood and cutting perfect joints. Shapers handle both straight and curved cuts. Straight cuts on the edges of most workpieces should always be guided by a fence. Curved cuts can be performed freehand or using a template. Templates are simple to build and can be custom-made for the job at hand. The workpiece is fastened to the template with double-sided tape or toggle clamps. The template rides on the rub bearing while the cutter shapes the workpiece. Another option for curve-cutting is a shop-made jig. A V-block jig for circle cuts is shown on page 40.

With a drawer joint cutter installed on its spindle, a shaper can make quick work of cutting both parts of a drawer joint. Featuring interlocking tongues and grooves and twice the gluing surface of a simple butt joint, the drawer joint is simple but strong.

STRAIGHT CUTS

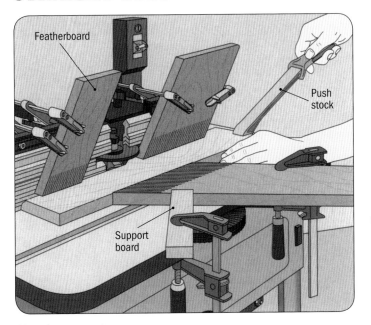

Featherboard

Push stock

Support board

Shaping an edge

Once the cutter and fence are set up, secure your workpiece with three featherboards. Clamp two featherboards to the fence, one on either side of the guard, and a third to the table in line with the cutter. Clamp a support board at a 90° angle to the featherboard for extra pressure. To make the cut, feed the workpiece into the cutter with both hands. Once the trailing end of the board reaches the table's edge, finish the pass using a push stick *(above)*, or by moving to the outfeed side of the table and pulling the stock past the cutter.

CUTTING A DRAWER JOINT

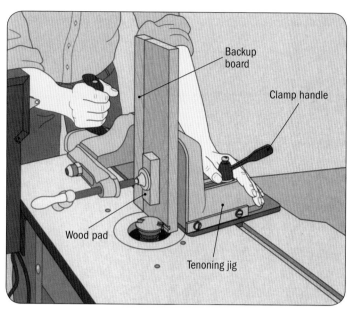

Backup board

Clamp handle

Wood pad

Tenoning jig

Cutting the drawer sides

For these cuts, the shaper is fitted with a router spindle and drawer joint bit. The joint is cut in two stages. The drawer sides are cut first, held upright in a tenoning jig. The drawer front and back are then cut face down in a miter gauge. Install a commercial tenoner on the table following the manufacturer's instructions; the model shown slides in the miter slot. Clamp the workpiece to the jig, protecting the stock with a wood pad. To prevent tearout, place a backup board behind the trailing edge of the workpiece. Follow the manufacturer's directions to adjust the jig for the depth and width of cut. Feed the work smoothly into the bit *(above)*.

CUTTING A DRAWER JOINT *(continued)*

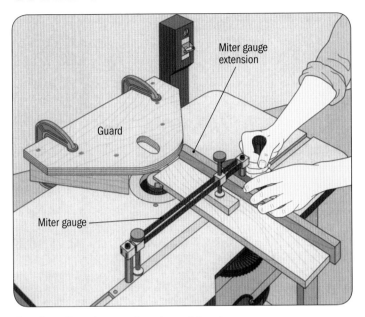

Cutting the drawer front and back

Remove the tenoner from the table and install a miter gauge equipped with hold downs. Also clamp a guard to the table to protect your hands from the bit; see page 29 for details on building the guard shown in this illustration. Protect the stock with a wood pad and clamp the workpiece to the miter gauge; position the board laterally on the jig for the width of cut. To provide additional support and reduce tearout, screw an extension board to the miter gauge. Slide the miter gauge and the stock as a unit into the cutter *(above)*. Test the fit of the joint and adjust the height of the bit, if necessary. If you want the drawer front to overhang the sides, you will need to make a few passes, increasing the width of cut slightly each time. Clamp a stop block to the extension board for repeat cuts.

LOCK MITER JOINT

Also known as a drawer lock joint, the lock miter is often used to assemble drawers. The joint features identical cuts in the mating boards, one in a board end and the other along the joining face. Both cuts are produced on a router table with the same bit. Because the lock miter is suitable with plywood, it is a good alternative to dovetails in such situations.

ROUTING A LOCK MITER

Making the cuts

Install a lock miter bit in your router and mount the tool in a table. Attach a notched auxiliary fence *(page 24)* and screw an extension board to the miter gauge. Set the bit height so the uppermost cutter is centered on the board end with the workpiece flat on the table.

Miter gauge extension

Auxiliary fence

ROUTING A LOCK MITER *(continued)*

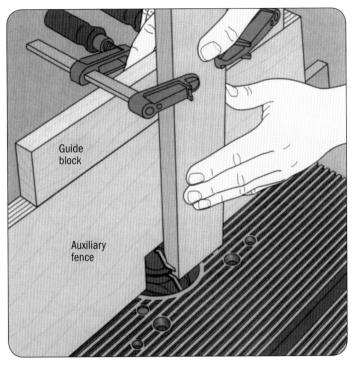

Guide block

Auxiliary fence

Position the fence so the bit will dado the stock without shortening it. Holding the workpiece against the fence and the miter gauge extension, feed the stock into the bit *(left)*. To cut the mating piece, clamp a guide block to it to ride along the top of the fence. Then feed the board on end into the cutter, keeping it flush against the fence with one hand while pushing it and the guide block forward with the other hand *(above)*.

PROFILING JIG

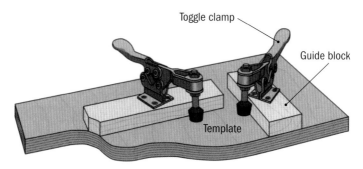

Toggle clamp

Guide block

Template

A profiling jig like the one shown above is a timesaving device for shaping several copies of the same curved pattern. The jig features a template of the shape you wish to reproduce. Clamp your stock atop the template, which will follow a rub bearing on the spindle, enabling the cutting edge to reproduce the pattern on the workpiece.

Make the template from a piece of ¾-inch plywood that is larger than the workpiece to provide a bearing surface before and after the cut. Cut the pattern with a band saw or a saber saw, then carefully sand the edges that will ride along the rub bearing. The template must be smooth since any imperfections will be transferred to your stock. Next, cut your workpieces roughly to size, oversizing the edge to be shaped by about ⅛ inch. Position the workpiece on the template, aligning the cutting mark on the edge to be shaped with the curved edge of the template. Using a pencil, outline the workpiece on the surface of the template. Fasten two guide blocks to the template from underneath with countersunk screws, lining up the edges of the blocks with the marked outline. To complete the jig, screw a toggle clamp to each guide block.

PROFILING JIG *(continued)*

Rub bearing

Cutter

Install a rub bearing and a straight cutter on the shaper. Adjust the height of the cutter so it will shape the full width of the workpiece; the rub bearing should be the same diameter as the cutter. Secure the workpiece on the jig, making sure to butt the stock flush against the guide blocks. Set the jig on the table and adjust the spindle height so the cutting edges will shape the entire edge of the workpiece. Also, make sure the template and the rub bearing are aligned.

To make the cut, turn on the shaper with the jig and workpiece clear of the cutter. Holding the toggle clamps, feed the workpiece into the cutter *(above).* Apply slight pressure to press the template against the rub bearing. Keep the template in contact with the bearing throughout the operation.

SHAPING WITH A TEMPLATE

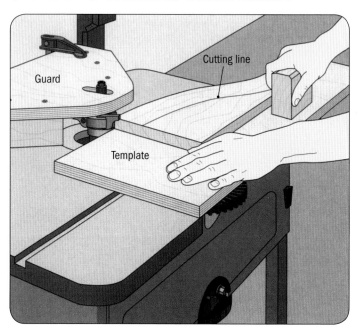

Cutting line

Guard

Template

Setting up and starting the cut

Build a template as you would a profiling jig (page 36); rather than edge
blocks and toggle clamps, this template has a 2-by-4 handle screwed
to it from underneath. Bevel the upper edges of the block for comfort.
Clamp a guard to the table to cover the cutter. Then cut the workpiece
roughly to size, making it several inches larger than you need so it
can be screwed to the template. Locate the screw holes in the waste
section you will cut away after the shaping operation is completed.
Start the cut as you would with the profiling jig, gripping the template
handle with your right hand to feed the workpiece and applying lateral
pressure with your left hand to keep the template flush against the rub
bearing (above).

SHAPING WITH A TEMPLATE *(continued)*

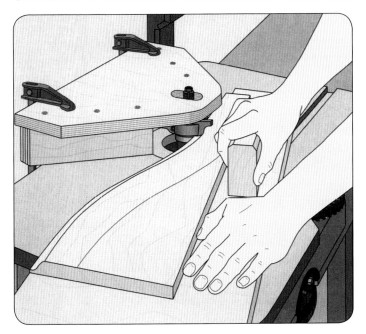

Completing the cut

Continue feeding with your right hand while using your left hand to keep
the template in contact with the rub bearing; the template should ride
along the bearing as the cutter shapes the workpiece. As the trailing end
of the stock reaches the cutter, gradually slide your left hand toward the
back of the workpiece *(above)*, maintaining pressure against the rub
bearing until the template clears the cutter. Once you have finished the
cut, unscrew the workpiece from the template and trim the waste.

A JIG FOR CIRCLE CUTS

Shaping circular work freehand on the shaper can be a risky job. One way to make the task safer and more accurate is to use a V-block jig like the one shown at right to help guide the cut; build the device from a piece of ¾-inch plywood.

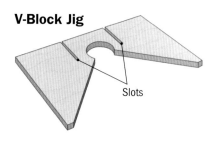

V-Block Jig

Slots

For most shapers, cut the jig about 24 inches long and 14 inches wide. To customize the jig for your shaper, hold it above the table flush with the back edge and mark the location of the spindle on the surface. Cut a right-angle wedge out of the jig, locating the apex of the angle at your marked point. Then cut a circle out of the jig centered on the apex; the hole should be large enough to accommodate the largest cutter you plan to use with the jig. Rout two slots into the back edge of the jig on either side of the hole—about 5 inches long and ½ inch wide—to line up with the holes in the shaper table for the fence locking rods.

Position the jig on the table, centering the bit in the hole. Seat the workpiece in the jig, butting it against both sides of the V, and adjust the jig and workpiece until the width of cut is set correctly. Tighten the fence locking handles to clamp the jig in place. You may want to make a test cut on a scrap piece to be certain that the depth and width of cut are correct.

A JIG FOR CIRCLE CUTS *(continued)*

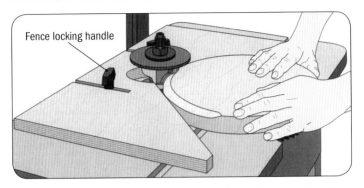

Fence locking handle

To use the jig, turn on the shaper and butt the workpiece against the outfeed side of the V. Slowly pivot the stock into the cutter until it rests firmly in the jig's V, moving it against the direction of cutter rotation to prevent kickback *(above)*. Continue rotating the workpiece until the entire circumference has been shaped, keeping the edge in contact with both sides of the jig throughout the cut.

FREEHAND SHAPING

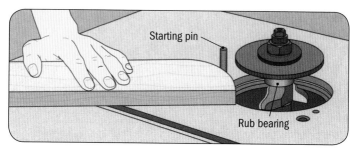

Starting pin

Rub bearing

Setting up the cut

Reverse the direction of cutter rotation to clockwise and place the
starting pin in its hole on the infeed side of the table. This will now be
the left-hand side. (For this cut, the rub bearing is mounted on the
spindle above the cutter, since the bottom portion of the workpiece's
edge is to be shaped.) Turn on the shaper and butt the leading end of
the stock against the starting pin (above).

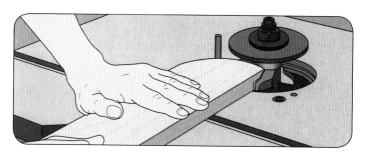

Starting the cut

Bracing the workpiece against the starting pin, pivot the stock into the
cutter (above). As the cutter bites into the stock, it tends to kick the
workpiece toward you; be sure to hold the board firmly. Once the workpiece
is in contact with both the starting pin and the rub bearing, slowly swing it
away from the pin while keeping it pressed against the rub bearing.

FREEHAND SHAPING *(continued)*

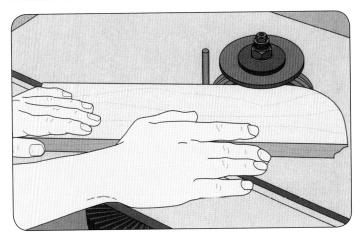

Completing the cut

Continue feeding the workpiece, maintaining constant pressure against the rub bearing *(above)*. Keep your hands well away from the edge of the workpiece being shaped. Once the cut is finished, slowly pull the stock away from the rub bearing and the cutter.

CHAPTER 5:

Vacuum Jigs

The vacuum system shown here is an excellent way to anchor featherboards to work tables and fasten templates to workpieces. The system is more convenient than conventional clamping and offers as much holding power without risking damage to stock. The limitation is that mating surfaces must be flat and smooth.

To set up a vacuum system, you need the parts shown in the photo at right. The tape is fastened to the underside of the featherboard or template, creating a cavity. The hose from the pump is inserted in a hole in the featherboard or template. When the jig is placed on the surface, the pump sucks the air from the cavity, producing a vacuum.

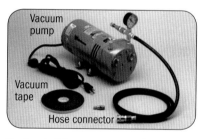

Vacuum pump

Vacuum tape

Hose connector

The heart of the vacuum system is the pump, here a ⅓ horsepower oil-less model, which draws air at a maximum of 4.5 cubic feet per minute. The hose features a quick coupler that attaches to a connector that is screwed into a hole through the template or featherboard. You will also need to use vacuum tape or closed-cell foam weatherstripping as a gasket to seal the cavity between template and workpiece or featherboard and work table.

A VACUUM FEATHERBOARD

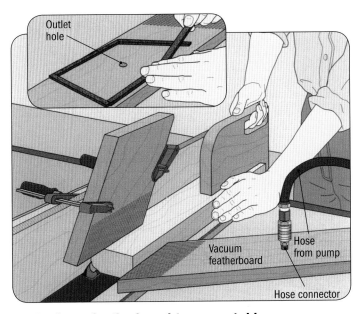

Outlet hole

Vacuum featherboard

Hose from pump

Hose connector

Anchoring a featherboard to a saw table

Bore an outlet hole through the center of the featherboard. The hole's diameter should be slightly less than that of the threaded end of the hose connector you will use. Next, apply four strips of closed-cell vacuum tape to the underside of the featherboard, forming a quadrilateral with no gaps *(inset)*. Screw the hose connector into the outlet hole on the top face of the featherboard; use a wrench as shown opposite. To set up the vacuum jig, place the featherboard on the saw table—for the molding cut shown, it is positioned to press the workpiece against the fence. Make certain the tape strips are flat on the table. Snap the quick coupler at the end of the vacuum pump hose onto the hose connector and turn on the pump. Air pressure will anchor the featherboard to the table as you feed the workpiece through the cut *(above)*.

VACUUM TEMPLATE ROUTING

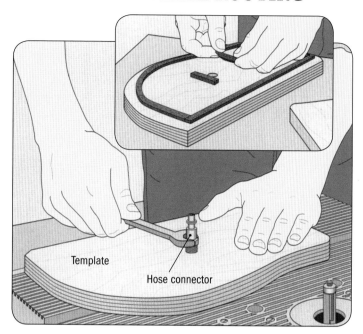

Template

Hose connector

Installing the tape and connector

A vacuum provides an effective alternative to double-sided tape for
fastening a plywood template atop a workpiece. Once your template
is the proper size, trace its pattern on your stock and cut out most of
the waste from your workpiece, leaving about ⅛ inch overhanging the
template. Bore the outlet hole through the middle of the template and
apply vacuum tape along the perimeter of its underside; make sure
there are no gaps between adjacent pieces of tape. With thin stock, add
two thin strips of tape on either side of the outlet hole to prevent the
vacuum pressure from pulling the middle of the workpiece against the
template *(inset)*. Attach the hose connector to the top of the template in
the outlet hole *(above)*.

VACUUM TEMPLATE
ROUTING *(continued)*

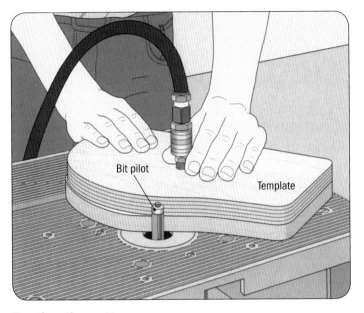

Bit pilot

Template

Routing the pattern

Install a piloted flush-trimming bit in a router, mount the tool in a table, and adjust the cutting height so the bit will shape the entire edge of the workpiece. Place the template tape-side-down centered on top of the workpiece. Attach the vacuum hose to the connector and switch on the pump to clamp the two boards together. Turn on the router and ease the stock into the bit until the template contacts the bit pilot *(above)*. Complete the cut, keeping the workpiece flat on the router table and the edge of the template pressed flush against the pilot; move against the direction of bit rotation.

CHAPTER 6:

Frame-and-Panel Doors

Frame-and-panel construction has been popular with woodworkers for close to 500 years. It offers a solution to the problem of wood movement by allowing the panel to expand and contract freely as ever-changing moisture levels in the air cause wood to swell and shrink. Humidity levels in centrally heated houses can range from 10 percent in winter to 85 percent in summer.

A frame-and-panel assembly comprises two horizontal members—rails—and two vertical stiles, all locked together with strong joints. The following pages will show you how to cut the commonly used cope-and-stick joint.

This frame-and-panel door features a sturdy frame of rails and stiles encasing a decorative floating panel. The contrast between the walnut panel and ash frame makes this door all the more striking.

A COPE-AND-STICK FRAME

Setting up for the cope cuts

Start by making the cope cuts into the ends of the rails. Install a coping cutter and ring guard on the shaper, then build a coping jig. The simple jig is made from four pieces: a ¾-inch

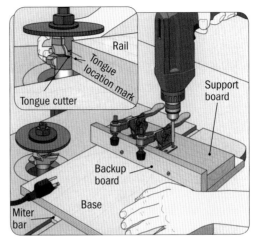

Rail

Tongue location mark

Tongue cutter

Support board

Backup board

Base

Miter bar

plywood base sized to fit between the spindle and the front edge of the table, a miter bar screwed to the bottom of the base that rides in the miter slot, a 2-by-4 support board fastened atop the base flush with the back edge, and a plywood backup board screwed to the support board. To prevent tearout on the workpiece, the backup board should extend beyond the base to the desired width of cut. To complete the jig, screw two toggle clamps to the support board *(above)*. Countersink all your fasteners. To set the cutter to the correct height, mark two lines for the tongue location on the rail; the tongue should be centered between the faces of the board. Position the jig on the table and set the workpiece on the base. Adjust the cutter height to align the tongue cutter between the marks *(inset)*.

A COPE-AND-STICK FRAME *(continued)*

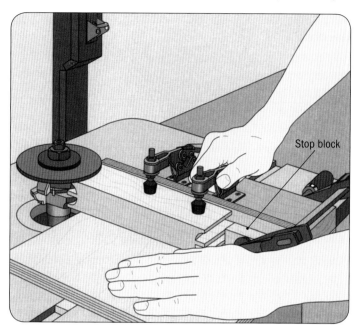

Stop block

Making the cope cuts in the rails

Position the workpiece on the jig base flush with the end of the backup board so the cutter will shape the entire board end, then use the toggle clamps to secure the stock in place. Butt a stop block against the opposite end of the workpiece and clamp it in place. Turn on the shaper and feed the workpiece into the cutter with one hand gripping a toggle clamp and the other braced on the jig base. Remove the workpiece, turn it around in the jig and repeat the cut to shape the tongue at the other end *(above)*.

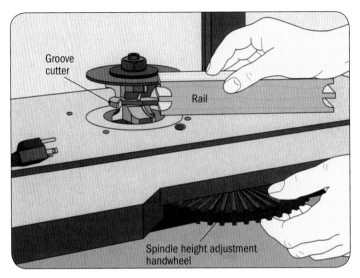

Groove
cutter

Rail

Spindle height adjustment
handwheel

Adjusting the height of the sticking bit

Once all the cope cuts are made, remove the coping cutter and install
a stick cutter set on the shaper. Be sure the groove cutter is the same
thickness as the tongue left by the cope cuts. This setup will shape the
edges of the stiles with a decorative profile and cut grooves for the rails
and the panels in one step. To set the cutting height, butt the end of one
of the completed rails against the stick cutter, then adjust the height of the
spindle so that the groove cutter is level with the tongue on the rail *(above)*.

Making the stick cuts

For the door shown at far right, with straight stiles, one straight-edged rail, and one curved rail, install the fence on the table for the straight cuts. Set the cutting width for a full cut—one that will shape the entire edge of each

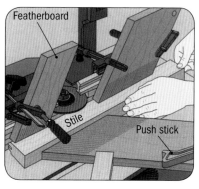

board. To secure the stock, clamp two featherboards to the fence and one to the table *(top)*. When feeding the workpiece into the cutter, use a push stick to complete the pass. To make the cut on the curved edge

of the top rail, remove the fence and build a profiling jig based on the model shown on page 36 to guide the piece. Install a rub bearing on the spindle and adjust the height of the cutter to accommodate the thickness of the jig. Feed the rail into the cutter, holding the jig's toggle clamps firmly *(bottom)*.

MAKING A RAISED PANEL

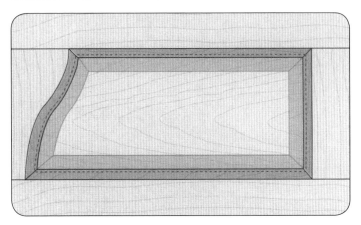

Cutting the panel to size

Assemble the frame dry and measure the opening between the rails and stiles. Add ½ inch to each of the dimensions to allow for the ¼ inch along the panel edges that will fit into the frame grooves *(above)*. For the curved top edge of the panel, outline the profile of the curved rail on the stock, then draw a parallel line offset from the first by ¼ inch. (The dotted lines in the illustration represent the actual edges of the panel; the solid lines represent the frame opening.) Make the straight cuts to size the panel on the table saw, ripping first, then crosscutting. Cut the curved top of the panel on the band saw.

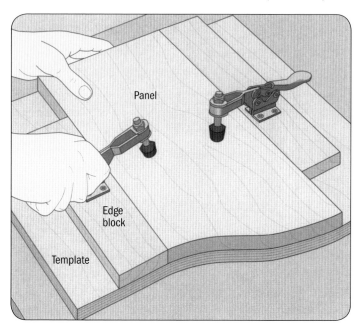

Setting up a panel-raising jig

Build a jig to guide the panel into the cutter safely and accurately. The jig consists of a template of ¾-inch plywood, cut to the same length as the panel, but about 12 inches wider to accommodate edge blocks; reproduce the curve of the panel's edge on the template. Center the panel on the template, then butt edge blocks against the panel and screw them to the template; to reduce tearout, the blocks should extend to the end of the template on the outfeed side of each cut. Screw a toggle clamp onto each edge block and secure the panel to the jig, making sure its ends are flush with the template ends *(above)*. (You may wish to make a test cut on a scrap piece, test its fit in the panel, and adjust the cutter height, if necessary.)

MAKING A RAISED PANEL *(continued)*

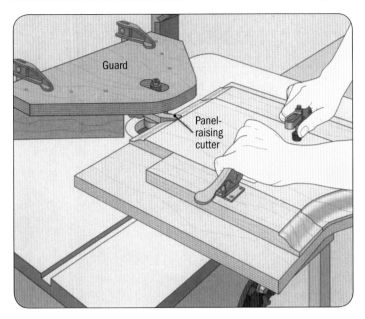

Raising the panel ends

Install a rub bearing and a panel-raising cutter on the shaper spindle. Adjust the cutting height to make a partial cut. (Do not attempt to raise the panel ends with one cut. You will need to make two or more passes, test-fitting after each cut until the panel fits properly into the rails.) Clamp a guard to the table to protect your hands from the cutter. Turn on the shaper, butt the template against the rub bearing, and feed the curved edge of the panel into the cutter, holding the jig firmly with both hands. Turn the jig around and repeat the procedure to raise the other end of the panel. Make successive passes, lowering the cutter until the panel fits in its mating groove *(above)*.

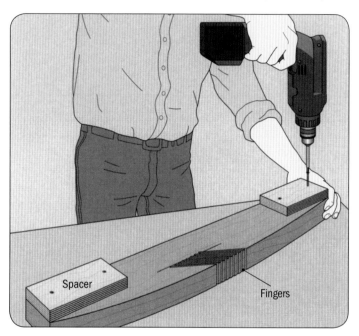

Spacer

Fingers

Making a featherboard for the straight cuts

To raise the sides of the panel safely, build an extra-wide featherboard. It will not only press the panel against the table, but also shield your fingers from the cutter. Cut a 2-by-4 to the length of your fence. Set the board against the fence and use a pencil to outline the location of the cutter on it. Then use the band saw to cut a series of ¼-inch-wide slots at a 30° to 45° angle within the outline, creating a row of sturdy but pliable fingers. Also curve the bottom edge of the featherboard so that only the fingers contact the panel during the shaping operation. Screw two spacers to the back face of the featherboard to enable the jig to clear the cutter; countersink the fasteners *(above)*.

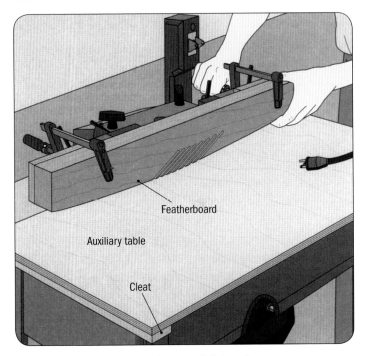

Featherboard

Auxiliary table

Cleat

Setting up the shaper for straight cuts

To avoid having to adjust the spindle height for shaping the panel
sides, install an auxiliary plywood table on the shaper that is the same
thickness as the profiling jig template you used to raise the ends
(page 36). Attach a cleat to each end of the plywood piece to hold it
snugly in place. Clamp the featherboard to the fence *(above)* so it will
apply pressure on the panel as you make the pass. Advance the fence
and featherboard away from the rub bearing on the first pass so you
remove only a portion of the waste.

MAKING A RAISED PANEL *(continued)*

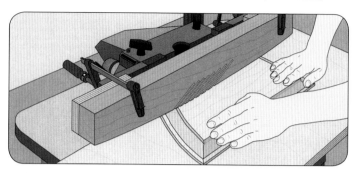

Raising the panel sides

Turn on the shaper and use your right hand to slowly feed the workpiece into the cutter; use your left hand to keep the panel against the fence. Turn the panel around and repeat the cut to shape the other side of the panel *(above)*. Move the fence closer to the rub bearing and shape both sides of the panel again. Make as many passes as necessary—two or three are usually sufficient—until the fence and rub bearing are aligned; this final pass will give you the full width and depth of cut.

ASSEMBLING THE DOOR

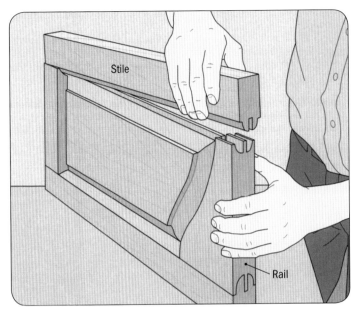

Stile

Rail

Test assembling and gluing up the pieces

Join a rail and a stile, then seat the panel between them. Set the stile on a work surface and add the second rail and stile *(above)*. Mark all the joints with a pencil to help you assemble the pieces when you apply the glue in the final assembly. The panel should fit snugly but easily. If it is too tight, make another light pass on the shaper along the ill-fitting edge or end. Assemble the door again. Once you are satisfied with the fit, apply glue to all the contacting surfaces of the frame. Do not spread any adhesive in the panel grooves; the panel must be free to move within the frame. Glue up the door, securing it with bar clamps.

Windows

The window sash shown here consists of two vertical stiles, two horizontal rails, a median rail, and two mullions that divide the sash vertically. The pieces are connected by cope-and-stick joints cut on a shaper. The joints between the stiles and rails are reinforced by splines. To size your stock, make the stiles equal to the height of the opening for the sash. For the rail length, take the width of the opening and subtract twice the stile width. Then add twice the depth of the coping cuts you will make. If, for example, the width of the window opening is 32 inches, the stiles are 3¼ inches wide, and the depth of the coping cuts is ¼ inch, each rail should be 26 inches long. You can also make the bottom rail wider than the other pieces to accommodate handles. To determine the length of each mullion, take the height of the opening and subtract the width of the three rails. Then add four times the depth of the coping cuts. Divide the total by two.

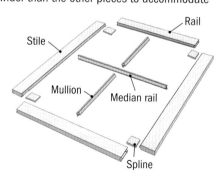

Rail

Stile

Mullion

Median rail

Spline

ASSEMBLING THE SASH

Paired with a shop-made mortising jig, a router cuts a mortise in one of the stiles of a window sash. The jig ensures that the mortise is centered on the edge of the stock. A matching mortise will be cut in the end of the adjoining rail and a spline will reinforce the joint between the two pieces.

ASSEMBLING THE SASH *(continued)*

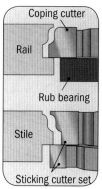

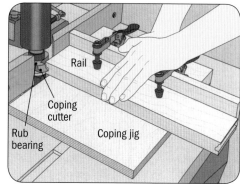

Making the coping cuts

As shown above at left, the joinery for the rails and stiles is done by matching cutters on the shaper. The coping cutter is used on the ends of all rails and mullions. The sticking cutter shapes the inside edges of the sash pieces. To set the height of the coping cutter, first install the sticking cutter in the shaper and adjust its height so the top of the cutter is level with one of the sash pieces set face down on the table. Make a cut in a test piece the same thickness as the sash stock. Then install the coping cutter and rub bearing on the shaper and butt the cut end of the test piece against the cutter to set its height. For the coping cuts, position the fence slightly behind the rub bearing and build a coping jig *(page 49)*. Use the jig to feed both ends of the rails into the cutter *(above, right)*. To cope the end of the median rail and mullions, shape a wide piece and rip the widths you need on the table saw.

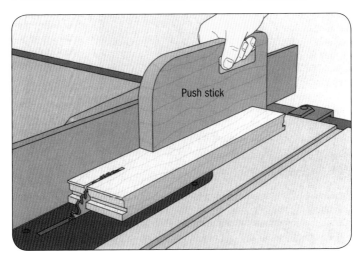

Push stick

Ripping the median rail and mullions

Once you have made the coping cuts on two wide boards for the median rail and mullions, position the table saw rip fence for cutting the median rail—typically one-third the width of the stiles. Feed the board into the blade with a push stick *(above)*. Reposition the fence for the mullions and cut them from the other board the same way.

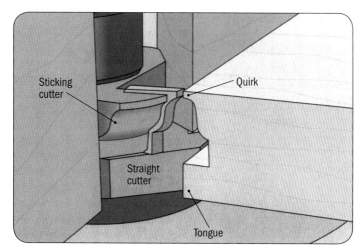

Sticking cutter

Quirk

Straight cutter

Tongue

Setting up the sticking cutter

Once all the rails and mullions are prepared, remove the coping cutter and rub bearing from the shaper and install a sticking cutter set. The one shown features a straight cutter, which should be the same width as the tongue left by the coping cuts. This setup will shape the inside edge of all the sash pieces and cut rabbets to support the glass. Butt one of the rails against the bit to set the height of the sticking cutter *(above)*; the tip at the top of the cutter should be aligned with the lip, or quirk, at the top of the coped end.

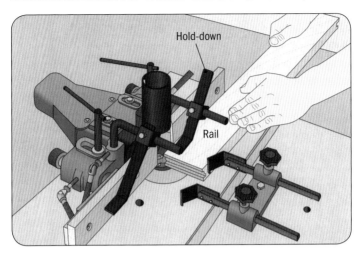

Hold-down

Rail

Making the sticking cuts

To make the sticking cuts, adjust the shaper's fence to make a full cut in the edge of the stock; the cutter should just touch the widest point of the workpiece. Also install commercial hold-downs on the shaper's fence and table to secure the stock during the cuts and prevent kickback and chatter. Then, make the sticking cuts in the inside edges of the rails and stiles, feeding the stock at a steady rate *(above)* and use a push stick to finish the cuts. Repeat this process for the median rail and mullions but this time shaping both edges of the piece.

7: WINDOWS

Assembling the Sash

ASSEMBLING THE SASH *(continued)*

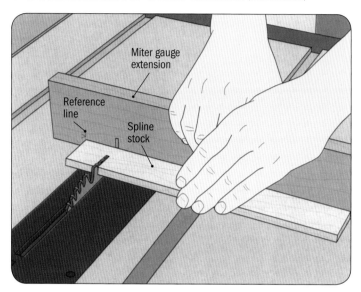

Miter gauge extension

Reference line

Spline stock

Strengthening the corner joints

Reinforce the joints between the stiles and the top and bottom rails with splines. Start by routing mortises for the splines in the ends of the rails and the inside edges of the stiles. The spline should fit the mortises snugly and be shorter than the combined depth of the two mating mortises. You can cut all the splines from a single board. To do the job on the table saw, screw a wooden extension to the miter gauge. Ensure that all the splines will be the same length by marking a reference line on the extension. Align the end of the board with the line and hold its edge against the extension to cut each spline *(above)*. For maximum strength, cut the splines so their grain will run in the same direction as the grain of the rails.

ASSEMBLING THE SASH *(continued)*

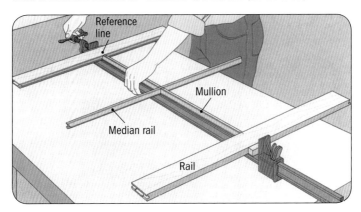

Reference line

Mullion

Median rail

Rail

Gluing the mullions to the rails

Glue up the frame in two steps. Start by gluing the rails and mullions together, as shown above, then add the stiles. Test-fit the pieces, marking reference lines across the joints with the mullions to help you align the parts during glue-up. For the rails and mullions, apply glue to the contacting surfaces of the boards. Assemble the pieces and install a bar clamp to secure the mullions to the top and bottom rails *(above)*; use wood pads to protect the stock.

Assembling the Sash

ASSEMBLING THE SASH *(continued)*

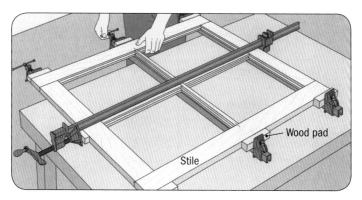

Wood pad

Stile

Gluing the stiles to the rails

Insert the splines in the rails and apply glue to the joints between the rails and stiles. Spread glue in the mortises and onto the splines. Turn the window over and secure the stiles in place with bar clamps *(above)*. Align a clamp with each rail, ensuring that the ends of the stiles are flush with the edges of the rails. Use wood pads to protect the stock. As soon as the clamps are tight, check the assembly for square by measuring the sash from corner to corner in both directions. The two diagonals should be equal. If not, readjust the clamping pressure slightly until the sash is square.

INSTALLING THE GLASS AND GLASS-STOP MOLDING

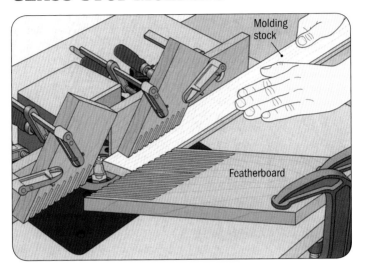

Molding stock

Featherboard

Making glass-stop molding

Glass-stop molding will hold the glass against the rabbets in the window sash. To prepare the molding with a router, install a decorative molding bit in the tool and mount it in a table. Shape both edges of a wide board long enough to yield all the molding you will need, then rip the molding strips from the stock. Use three featherboards to support the workpiece during the cut: two clamped to the fence on either side of the bit and one clamped to the table. Feed the board into the cutter while keeping it flush against the fence; finish the pass with a push stick. Repeat to shape the other edge *(above)*. Cut the molding off the board on the table saw, then saw it to length, making 45° miter cuts at the end of each piece.

INSTALLING THE GLASS AND GLASS-STOP MOLDING *(continued)*

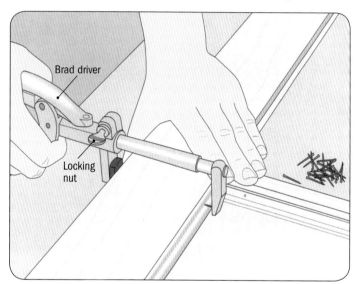

Brad driver

Locking nut

Installing the glass and the molding

Set the sash and glass on a work surface, then place the molding in position. Bore a pilot hole every 6 inches, insert a finishing nail into each hole, and drive it home. To use a brad driver, as shown above, adjust the jaws against the sash and the nail, then tighten the locking nut. Holding the sash steady, squeeze the jaws to set the nail.

ShopTip

Installing the molding with a hammer
If you are using a hammer to nail glass-stop molding in place, protect the glass by placing a piece of cardboard on it as you drive each nail, as shown here.

CHAPTER 8:
Entry Doors

A shaper is invaluable for making frame-and-panel doors. Fitted with cope-and-stick cutter sets, it will prepare the stiles and rails for assembly, cutting grooves for the "floating" panels that fill the frame and carving a decorative molding along the inside edges of the frame at the same time. Then, equipped with a panel-raising bit, the shaper can form bevels on the panel edges, as shown in the photo above. The large shop-made featherboard clamped to the shaper's fence protects the user from the cutter and holds the panel flat on the table. Step-by-step instructions for building a six-panel Federal-style door are provided on the following pages.

MAKING AN ENTRY DOOR

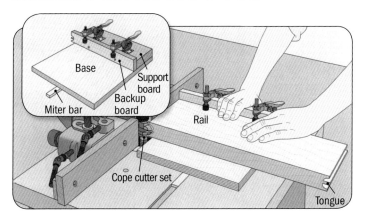

Base
Support board
Backup board
Miter bar
Rail
Cope cutter set
Tongue

Making cope cuts on the rails

A six-panel door features two stiles, a top and bottom rail, two median rails, and three mullions. Cut your stock to size, then install a coping cutter set and guard on the shaper. To feed the rails, build the coping jig shown in the inset. The jig consists of a plywood base, a miter bar screwed to the underside of the base, a 2-by-4 support board fastened flush with the back edge of the base, and a plywood backup board screwed to the support board. To prevent tearout on the rails, the backup board should support the workpiece for the full width of the cut. Screw two toggle clamps to the support board. Next, mark the tongue location on one of the rails, centered on the edge of the board. Position the jig on the shaper table, set one of the rails on the jig and adjust the cutter height to align the cutter with the tongue mark. Then clamp the rail to the jig, aligning the board end with the end of the backup board so the cutter will shape the entire edge. Now make the cut, pushing the jig across the table. Repeat the cut on the other end of the rail *(above)*, then make the cuts on both ends of the remaining rails and mullions.

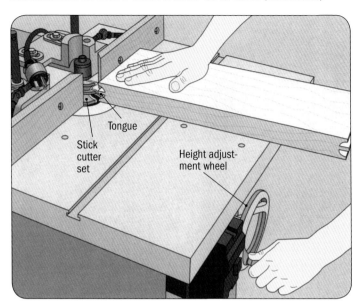

Tongue

Stick cutter set

Height adjustment wheel

Adjusting the stick cutter

Once all the cope cuts are made, replace the cope cutter with the matching stick cutter set. This setup will shape the edges of the stiles, mullions, and rails with a decorative profile while cutting grooves to accommodate the tongues and panels. To set the cutting height, butt the end of one of the coped rails against the stick cutter, then adjust the height of the spindle so the groove cutter is level with the tongue on the rail *(above)*.

MAKING AN ENTRY DOOR *(continued)*

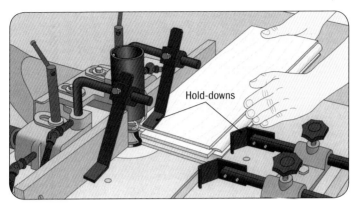

Hold-downs

Making the stick cuts

Adjust the fence to shape the entire edge of the stock. Also install commercial or shop-made hold-downs on the fence and shaper table to secure the stock through the cuts and prevent kickback. Shape both edges of the median rails and mullions, feeding the stock across the table with both hands *(above)*, but shape only the inside edges of the stiles and top and bottom rails.

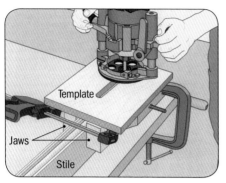 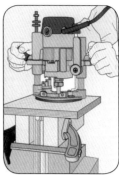

Routing mortises in the stiles and rails

Reinforce the joints between the stiles and rails with splines. To determine their locations, test-assemble the stiles and rails and mark the center of the joints between them. Take the assembly apart and secure a stile edge-up on a work surface. Use a router fitted with a mortising bit and a template guide to cut mortises for the splines. To guide the tool, build the jig shown above, made from a piece of ¾-inch plywood with a slot in the middle and two 2-by-4 jaws screwed to the bottom of the template to straddle the stile. The slot should be the size of the groove you wish to cut plus the diameter of the template guide you will attach to the router. Clamp the jig to the stile, then set the cutting depth to cut a 1½-inch-deep mortise in the stile. Turn on the router and make the cut, guiding the template guide along the inside edges of the jig slot *(above, left)*. Repeat the cut at the other end of the stile, at both ends of the other stile, and at the center of the median rails. Next, secure the rails end up and rout grooves in their ends the same way *(above, right)*.

MAKING AN ENTRY DOOR *(continued)*

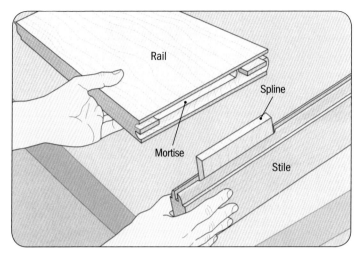

Test-fitting the joint

Once all the grooves are cut, make splines that fit the mortises and are shorter than the combined depth of two mortises. The grain of the splines should run in the same direction as the rails. Test fit one of the joints before glue-up *(above)*. The joint should fit together smoothly without binding. If the fit is too tight, trim the spline and test-fit the joint again. Finally, make reference marks on all the rails and stiles to help you assemble them properly during glue-up.

MAKING AN ENTRY DOOR *(continued)*

Raising the panels

To help you size the panels, assemble the door stiles, mullions, and rails, and measure the openings. Add ½ inch to each dimension to allow for the ¼ inch along the edge of the panel that will fit into the grooves. Cut the panels to size; your stock should be no thicker than the stock used for

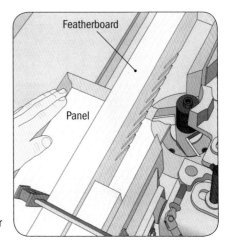

the stiles and rails. Install a panel-raising bit and matching rub bearing in the shaper, and adjust the fence even with the rub bearing. Then adjust the cutter height so the raised edges of the panels will penetrate the grooves by ¼ inch when the panel is cut on both sides. Clamp a wide featherboard to the shaper fence to shield you from the cutter and hold the panel flat on the shaper table. Feed each panel face-up into the cutter, using your left hand to keep the workpiece flush against the fence *(above)*. To prevent tearout, shape the panel ends first, then the sides. Once one side of the panel has been shaped, turn it end-for-end and repeat on the other edge. Then turn the panel over and repeat the series of cuts.

MAKING AN ENTRY DOOR *(continued)*

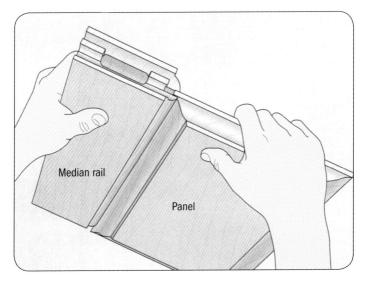

Median rail

Panel

Testing the fit of the panels

Once you have shaped the first panel, fit it into one of the grooves in a stile *(above)*. The pieces should fit together snugly, with the panel extending ¼ inch into the groove. If not, adjust the cutting height, repeat the cuts and test the fit again. Once you are satisfied with the fit, raise the remaining panels.

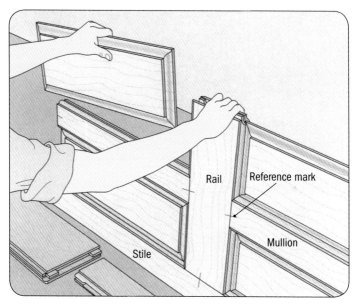

Rail

Reference mark

Mullion

Stile

Assembling the door

Lay out all the pieces of the door close at hand so that you can
assemble the door quickly before the glue begins to set. Start building
the door by setting a stile edge-up on the floor. Apply glue in the
mortises in the stile and its adjoining rails as well as on the splines. Do
not spread any glue in the panel grooves. Insert the splines in the stile
mortises and fit the rails in place. Use the reference marks you made
earlier to help you assemble the pieces properly. Tap the top ends of the
rails lightly with a mallet to close the joints. Now, seat panels between
the stiles and rails. Continue in this fashion, applying glue in the spline
grooves and on the splines and fitting the pieces in place *(above)* until
the door is assembled.

MAKING AN ENTRY DOOR *(continued)*

Clamping the door

Lay four bar clamps on the floor, one for each rail. Carefully lay the assembled door on the clamps so the bars of the clamps are aligned with the rails. To protect your stock, place wood pads the length of the door between the clamp

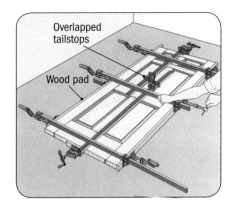

Overlapped tailstops

Wood pad

jaws and the door edges. Tighten the clamps just enough to close the joints. Then clamp the door from top to bottom along the mullions. If you do not have a clamp that is long enough to span the door, use two clamps, positioning them so that their tailstops contact each other near the middle of the door. Use shorter wood pads to protect the door from these clamp jaws. Install three more clamps across the top face of the door, aligning the bars with the top, bottom, and middle rail. Finish tightening all the clamps until glue squeezes out of the joints *(above)*. Then use a try square to check that the corners of the door are square; adjust the clamping pressure, if necessary. Once the glue has dried, use a paint scraper to remove any remaining adhesive. When the glue has cured, sand and finish the door.

CHAPTER 9:

Handrails

A handrail can be the most complex and decorative element of a staircase. But it also performs the more pedestrian—but vital—task of guiding the people who climb and descend the stairs. Whether a handrail is as elaborate as a curved assembly made from laminated strips of wood, or as simple as the straight example featured in this section, most building codes govern several aspects of its construction. For example, a handrail is usually required on any staircase with three or more treads. It is typically screwed or bolted to the newel posts and attached to the tops of the balusters. A rail should also typically not encroach more than 3½ inches into the minimum width of the staircase. Commercial rails and hardware for floating handrails generally satisfy building codes.

The handrail shown at right culminates in a spiral-shaped form, known as a volute, at the foot of the stairs.

HANDRAIL DESIGNS

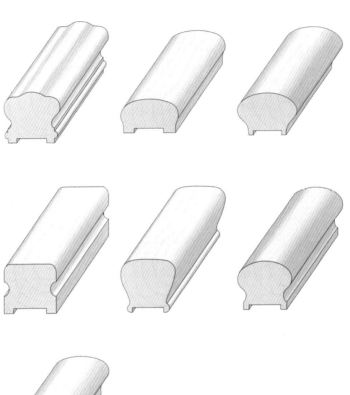

SHAPING A HANDRAIL

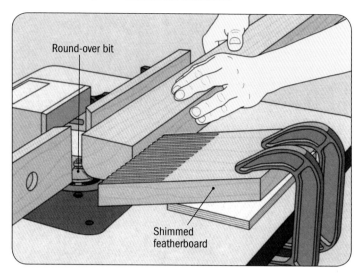

Round-over bit

Shimmed
featherboard

Routing the profile

Install a bit with the desired
top profile in your router
and mount the tool in a
table. In this example, a
round-over bit is shown.
Align the fence with the bit
pilot bearing. To support
the handrail as you shape

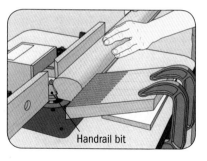

Handrail bit

it, clamp a featherboard to the table in line with the bit. Place a shim
under the featherboard so that the pressure is applied near the middle
of the stock. Feed the rail upside down, then turn it around and shape
the other edge of the top *(top)*. To form the side profile, replace the bit.
In this case, a specialized handrail bit is used. Feed the rail across the
table in two passes again, this time right side up *(bottom)*.

SHAPING A HANDRAIL *(continued)*

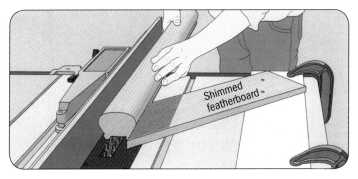

Shimmed
featherboard

Cutting the baluster groove in the handrail

To accommodate the top ends of the balusters, saw a groove down the middle of the handrail's underside. Install a dado blade, adjusting it as wide as possible; you will likely need more than one pass to cut the full width of the groove. Adjust the cutting height to about ¼ inch, then mark the groove in the center of the leading end of the stock. The width of the groove should be equal to the thickness of the balusters. Clamp a shimmed featherboard to the saw table in line with the dado head. Align one of the groove marks with the inside blade, butt the rip fence against the handrail and feed the stock into the cut. Turn the handrail around and repeat the cut *(above)*.

Shaping a Handrail

Index

Index